HENRY FORD

Mass Production and the Model T

Written by Véronique Van Driessche
Translated by Rebecca Neal

History 50MINUTES.com

50MINUTES.com
BECOME AN EXPERT
IN HISTORY
DARWIN'S THEORY OF EVOLUTION
George Washington
The Battle of Austerlitz
Neil Armstrong
The Six-Day War
The Fall of Constantinople
www.50minutes.com

HENRY FORD

KEY INFORMATION

- **Born:** 30 July 1863 in Greenfield Township, Michigan.
- **Died:** 7 April 1947 at Fair Lane, Dearborn, Michigan.
- **Famous inventions:**
  - The Ford Model T, generally considered to be the first affordable car
  - The moving assembly line
  - Fordism, a rationalised production method.
- **Impact of his inventions:**
  - Automobiles made accessible to all
  - The development of mass production
  - The appearance of a new social class following a rise in workers' salaries
  - The start of mass consumption.

INTRODUCTION

Although Henry Ford did not invent the petrol-powered car and was far from the only automobile producer in the early 20th century, he was different in that he understood that this invention would change the world. At a time when owning a car was a luxury reserved for the privileged few, he dreamed of making automobiles accessible and allowing every family to obtain one.

On 1 October 1908, the Model T, a small car produced by the Ford Motor Company, came out of the factory on Piquette Avenue in Detroit. Simple, sturdy and above all affordable, the Model T was so successful that over 15 million were sold between 1908 and 1927.

To achieve this, Ford revolutionised the process of automobile production by introducing the division of labour (each worker is assigned a single very specific task) and the moving assembly line (the product being put together moves automatically from one post to another, so that the workers no longer have to move around). In this way, he managed to reduce selling prices and double workers' salaries while maintaining the quality of the product. Subsequently, the principle of the assembly line was widely applied in industry, and contributed to the development of the mass production and mass consumption which characterised 20th-century society.

CONTEXT

THE INDUSTRIAL REVOLUTION AND THE MOVE TOWARDS PROGRESS

From the 19th century onwards, Western nations were working towards progress. Industrialisation and economic growth went hand in hand, fuelled by various technological innovations and the discovery of new energy sources. The change from a society which until that point had been mainly agricultural was so radical that it is generally described as the Industrial Revolution.

The First Industrial Revolution began in Britain in the second half of the 18th century, thanks to the growth of the metalworking and textile industries, the invention of the steam engine and coal mining. After centuries of traditional, small-scale production, Europe and then the world as a whole saw the development of large-scale production in specialised factories. The Panic of 1873, a financial crisis which resulted in a depression in Europe and North America, briefly interrupted this momentum, but growth resumed from 1880 onwards thanks to the Second Industrial Revolution. This new revolution was based on the innovations brought about by the use of electricity, gas and oil, as well as the chemical industry.

From then on, many businesses were founded and took advantage of the possibilities of each new sector (electricity, automobile, etc.), and the number of investors, who provided the necessary capital, rose considerably. Thanks to the growing wealth of the most industrialised countries and the extension of markets across the world, demand was constantly increasing. There was great enthusiasm for technology, which had provided light, the petrol engine, the telephone and the film projector. However, optimism and creativity once again ground to a halt in 1929, with the beginnings of a global economic crisis.

THE INVENTION OF THE AUTOMOBILE

Each Industrial Revolution was accompanied by a major change in the means of transport: after the miracle of the railways in the 19th century, the Second Industrial Revolution was the age of the automobile. However, this innovation did not come about overnight and was not the work of a single inventor. According to estimates, it took over 10 000 patents before the development of the cars we drive today.

From the steam engine to the combustion engine

The *fardier à vapeur* ("steam dray") designed by the French military engineer Nicolas-Joseph Cugnot (1725-1804) is generally described as the first automobile, meaning a vehicle which is self-powered and does not rely on animals to pull it. The *fardier à vapeur*, which was presented to the public on 23 October 1769, was an enormous three-wheeled cart powered by steam. It could reach speeds of 2.5 mph and travel for 15 minutes. Initially designed to transport cannons for the army, it was then adapted to seat four passengers.

Cugnot's *fardier à vapeur*, drawing by Louis Figuier

The period between 1820 and 1840 saw the creation of steam-powered stagecoaches, first in Britain, then in France and the USA. However, steam engines were heavy, inefficient and slow to start, making them unsuitable for road vehicles. A lighter and more efficient model was subsequently devised: the internal combustion engine, which works by burning gas very quickly to move a piston in a cylinder, in an identical process to that of the steam engine. The principle of internal combustion (as opposed to combustion outside the engine) allowed heat loss to be avoided, thus improving the output of the engine.

The first internal combustion engine, a two-stroke engine which ran on lighting gas, was built by the Belgian-born French engineer Étienne Lenoir (1822-1900) in 1860. It was not until the 1870s, when the American George Brayton (1830-1892) invented a carburettor which produced an efficient mixture of fuel and air, that this engine could run on petrol.

BLACK GOLD

Since the mid-19th century, oil had been extracted and refined in the USA to produce lighting oil and other derivatives, including tar, solvents and petrol. The development of the internal combustion engine at the end of the 19th century and the rapid spread of the automobile gave it an unexpected importance: this was the beginning of the black gold rush.

Towards the modern petrol engine

In 1862, the French engineer Alphonse Eugène Beau de Rochas (1815-1893) established the principles of a four-stroke engine (intake, compression, combustion and exhaust), which offered a higher output. The German engineer

Nikolaus Otto (1832-1891) took advantage of his idea, and in 1876 presented the first four-stroke internal combustion engine. Although this still ran on gas, it was behind most of the subsequent internal combustion engines and was widely used in factories and power stations.

A few years later, in 1885, the German engineer Karl Benz (1844-1929) designed and built the first automobile to incorporate Otto's four-stroke engine, which ran on petrol this time. He patented it on 29 January 1886. This three-wheeled car had a gearbox and a differential gear, and could reach speeds of 7.5 mph. He sold two of the vehicle, and for this reason is considered to be the founder of the automobile industry.

Karl Benz's car, dated 1886.

Also in 1885, another German engineer, Gottlieb Daimler (1834-1900), with the help of his partner Wilhelm Maybach (1846-1929), improved Otto's engine and patented what is now recognised as the prototype of the modern petrol engine. This small, light and quick engine was the first truly efficient internal combustion engine. On 8 March 1886,

Daimler installed his engine in a carriage, in this way creating the first four-wheeled automobile, and in 1890 he founded *Daimler-Motoren-Gesellschaft*, which produced his engines. Eleven years later, Maybach designed the first Mercedes.

Finally, in 1889, the French engineers René Panhard (1841-1908) and Émile Levassor (1843-1897) installed Daimler's engine in a four-seater car, which they sold from 1891 onwards. From then on, France was the leader in automobile construction for a time: in 1903, it produced 48% of the world's cars. However, it was in the USA that cars really became popular, thanks to Henry Ford.

BIOGRAPHY OF HENRY FORD

A LOVE FOR MACHINES

Ford was born on 30 July 1863 on his parents' farm in Greenfield Township, Michigan. He was the eldest of six children. His grandparents on his father's side were originally from Cork in Ireland, and had arrived in the USA in 1847.

The young Henry disliked both school and farm work. However, he was very good with machines and had a marked taste for independent learning. His favourite toys were tools and bits of machinery that he worked on. At the age of 12 he received a watch, which he took apart and put back together in order to understand how it worked. With training, he learnt to repair any watch, and even tried his hand at making them. One year later, he saw a steam-powered road vehicle for the first time. This made such an impression on him that, from then on, he developed a keen interest in automobile transport and made increasingly precise models. By the age of 15, he could put together and repair a steam engine.

In 1879, Ford left school and the family farm. He briefly worked at the Michigan Car Company, which produced railroad cars, before being taken on as an apprentice machinist with James F. Flower & Bros., which made pieces of machinery. Finally, he worked at the Detroit Dry Dock Engine Works, another machine shop. By night, he repaired watches in a jeweller's shop to pay his rent, and during his free time he worked on a range of mechanical experiments.

RETURN TO THE FARM AND HIS ELECTRIC PHASE

Between 1882 and 1891, he was back at his parents' farm, but never missed an opportunity to tinker with engines. In addition, for several summers in a row, he worked for the Westinghouse Electric Company, demonstrating and repairing steam engines used to transport heavy loads or power threshing machines. When he turned 21, his father game him a sizeable piece of land and he agreed to remain (albeit temporarily) on the farm. In 1885, he met Clara Bryant (1866-1950), the daughter of a local farmer, at a dance. He married her on 13 April 1888 and they had a son, Edsel (1893-1943). In order to provide for his family, Ford cut down and sold the wood on his land, then set up a sawmill and offered his services across the region.

However, as soon as he could, he continued his mechanical work in the workshop he had set up for himself. He still dreamed of constructing a road vehicle, but had come to understand that he could not rely on steam. In 1885, he was asked to repair an Otto gas engine, and, two years later, he made one himself to ensure that he had fully understood how it worked. Then, in 1890, he tackled the construction of a petrol engine.

In September 1891, Ford found work as an engineer and machinist at the Edison Illuminating Company in Detroit, and moved to the city with his wife. In 1893, he was promoted to Chief Engineer, which finally gave him the means and the time to do more work on his petrol engine with his friends.

On Christmas Eve of the same year, he managed to make it run on the kitchen sink. He finished his car in June 1896 and named it the Quadricycle, as it was mounted on four bicycle wheels. At that time, it was the only working automobile in Detroit. However, Ford sold it and built another one, which he completed in 1898. The following year, he left the Edison Illuminating Company in order to move into the automobile industry.

Photograph of Ford in his first car, taken in 1896.

HENRY FORD AND THOMAS EDISON

In 1896, Ford met Thomas Edison (1847-1931) for the first time at a convention on electricity in Atlantic City.

Ford talked to him about his petrol car, and Edison encouraged him to persevere with his experiments, predicting that he had a bright future ahead of him. The two men subsequently became close friends.

FIRST STEPS IN THE AUTOMOBILE INDUSTRY

The Detroit Automobile Company, the first automobile company in the city, was founded on 5 August 1899 to sell vehicles with Ford's engine. Ford was appointed chief engineer. However, investors were looking for quick profit and wanted to produce the cars, which proved to be too expensive and of poor quality, as quickly as possible. Consequently, the company was dissolved in January 1901.

To make himself known, Ford began taking part in automobile racing. He and his friends built a powerful car which won a 10-mile race against the local champion on 10 October 1901. This victory gave his investors renewed confidence in him, and on 30 November 1901 they came together to support a new company, the Henry Ford Company. Once again, Ford was chief engineer. Nonetheless, the same problem resurfaced: the investors did not share Ford's aims, and on 10 March 1902 he left the company, which was then renamed the Cadillac Automobile Company.

He then joined forces with a local cycling champion, Tom Cooper (1874-1906), and built two 80-horsepower racing cars, the 999 and the Arrow. The cars were so powerful that the two men did not dare to drive them themselves, so they asked a very fast amateur cyclist, Barney Oldfield (1878-1946), to take the wheel instead. On 25 October 1902, the 999 won the Manufacturer's Challenge Cup and its driver continued with his career as an automobile racer.

Photograph of the 999 model with Barney Oldfield in the driver's seat and Ford standing next to him, 1902.

THE STORY OF THE FORD MOTOR COMPANY

The Ford Motor Company began operating in November 1902 and was incorporated on 16 June 1903, with the main aim of designing a light and affordable automobile. Initially, Ford was the vice-president and chief engineer, while 12 shareholders had 510 shares between them, for $28 000 capital. The first cars went on sale in July 1903, and by the following year the Ford Motor Company was thriving. This marked the beginning of an extraordinary rise, the main stages of which were the launch of the Model T in 1908 and the setting up of the first mobile assembly line in 1913.

Photograph of the first Ford assembly line, 1913.

Although he had already been the company's president and majority shareholder since 1906, in 1919 Ford bought all the remaining stock for over $100 million, making him the sole owner. Officially, he named his son Edsel president and retired, but in reality he continued to run the company.

By 1922, half the cars in America were Ford Model Ts, which were sold for under $300 dollars each. However, over time the brand diversified its products. The Fordson tractor came out in October 1917, and by the 1920s accounted for 75% of the tractors sold in the USA. 1925 also saw the launch of an aeronautics branch, with the creation of the Ford Trimotor three-engined aircraft, as well as airports and hotels. However, this adventure came to an end with the Wall

Street Crash of 1929. Finally, during the two World Wars, the Ford factories supplied the American army, producing ships, bombers, Jeeps, aeroplane engines and combat tanks.

In 1927, sales of the Model T declined, while other car brands became increasingly popular. It was time to innovate and move to a new model. The Ford Model A came out in December of that year and remained competitive for four years. In 1932, Ford announced the introduction of a completely new eight-cylinder engine, the Ford V-8, which was light and inexpensive. However, this did not stop General Motor and Chrysler from staying ahead of the Ford Motor Company on the American market.

HIGHLY DIVERSIFIED ACTIVITIES

Contrary to what might be believed, Ford's activity was not confined to the automobile industry. Among other activities, he campaigned for the protection of birds (1913), which he liked to observe from his Fair Lane estate in Dearborn, collected and restored items relating to the industrialisation of the USA (1913 onwards), built a hospital (1915), sailed to Norway with fellow pacifists to try and put an end to the First World War (1915), opened schools (1916 and 1929), ran for the Senate (1918), created "village industries", small factories in the countryside where cars were made for part of the year while workers worked on the farm the rest of the time (1920), and organised educational camps for underprivileged children and war orphans (1938). He also set up the Ford Foundation in 1936, which went on to become one of the largest philanthropic organisations in the world.

During the interwar years, Ford revealed a very controversial side to his personality. Driven by profound anti-Semitism and a belief in a Jewish conspiracy seeking to control the world, between 1920 and 1927 he published a series of articles in the *Dearborn Independent*, a local newspaper that he had bought in 1918. He brought these articles together in a multivolume work, *The International Jew* (1920-1922), which reportedly had a significant impact in Germany and was one of the major sources of Hitler's (1889-1945) ideas. In May 1938, he was awarded the Grand Cross of the German Eagle, the highest Nazi decoration that could be granted to a foreigner and a clear indication of the admiration that his ideas were met with in Germany. It has even been claimed that Ford provided financial support to the Nazi Party, but this has never been proven.

When his son died in 1943, Ford once again became president of the company, in spite of his declining health and the fact that he had already suffered two strokes. Finally, after a third stroke in 1945, he passed the reins of the company to his grandson Henry Ford II. Ford died of a cerebral haemorrhage two years later, on 7 April 1947 at the age of 83, in his house at Fair Lane.

WORKING TOWARDS A UNIVERSAL CAR FOR EVERYONE

After his first encounter with an engine-powered road vehicle, Ford held firm in his belief that this invention could be made more accessible. When he entered the automobile industry, his only aim was to construct a universal car: simple, easy to drive and maintain, light but of excellent quality, and affordable.

FIVE YEARS OF EXPERIMENTATION

When it was first founded, the Ford Motor Company comprised seven workers who worked ten hours per day in a hired workshop on Mack Avenue, Detroit. As an engineer, Ford designed and repaired the machines in the factory, drew up plans for automobiles and engines, and filed patents for his inventions.

During the first year (1903-1904), the company produced the Ford Model A, a small two-cylinder car. Its basic model cost $850, and 1708 were sold. In spite of its price, which was still fairly high, the car was popular because it was sturdy, simple and functional.

A Ford Model A, dating from 1903.

During the second year (1904-1905), three models went on sale: the Model B, a four-cylinder passenger car (meaning that it had four or more seats), sold for $2000; the Model C, which was an improved version of the Model A and cost $900; and the Model F, another passenger car, which was priced at $1000 dollars. That year, 1695 cars were sold. In December 1904, production was moved to a new, larger factory on Piquette Avenue.

During the third year (1905-1906), the Model B and Model F continued to be produced, but sales levelled out at 1599 cars. In 1906-1907, Ford abandoned large cars and launched the Model N, a small touring car which cost between $600 and $750. It proved a bestseller, with 8453 sold in a single year. It was also sold in 1907-1908, along with the Model K, a large six-cylinder car which was priced at up to $2800. A total of 6398 cars were sold that year. The business was thriving, and Ford vehicles began to be sold in Europe.

Photograph of a couple in a Ford Model N, taken by William Creswell in 1906.

THE LAUNCH OF THE MODEL T

In August 1908, Ford finally announced the manufacture of the car he had been dreaming of, a simple car that responded to the needs of as many people as possible. This was the famous Model T, which came out in October of that year. It was the first car with interchangeable parts, meaning that the same chassis was used for passenger cars, small road cars and coupés, which were sold from $825. It was accompanied by two other models that year, but their sales were eclipsed by those of the Model T, which would subsequently be the only model produced. From 1914 onwards, it was only available in black, the cheapest and fastest-drying colour. Standardisation was taken to the limit, but new versions of the Ford Model T still appeared regularly in order to boost the market.

Ford posing next to the Model T, 1921.

The Model T was initially manufactured in the factory on Piquette Avenue, which produced 18 000 cars in 1909. However, this was not enough to meet the constantly increasing demand, so production moved to the Highland Park Ford Plant, to the north of Detroit, on 1 January 1910. This new factory produced 70 000 Model Ts in 1911 and over 170 000 the following year.

THE SELDEN CASE

Since 1906, Ford had been engaged in legal proceedings against the patent filed by George B. Selden (1846-1922). Selden, a patent lawyer and inventor, claimed to have filed a patent in 1879 which gave him a monopoly over all vehicles using an internal combustion engine, and because of this claimed royalties from all automobile manufacturers. Mass production could not really begin until Ford had won the case in 1911.

RATIONALISED PRODUCTION

To respond to rising demand and reduce the price of cars while covering the costs of the mechanics and maintaining the same quality, Ford and his engineers constantly strove to increase productivity in their factories.

On the one hand, the construction of the parts needed for the vehicles was mechanised as much as possible. New machines were invented to make them, and engineers designed parts that were as simple as possible, standardised and interchangeable, so that they could be produced in very large numbers. On the other hand, methods of automobile assembly underwent a number of adjustments with the aim of boosting the output of workers. Specifically, Ford applied the theories of Frederick Winslow Taylor (1856-1915), who, at the beginning of the 20th century, had defined a method of work organisation which he called scientific management, and which became known as Taylorism. The idea was to break the assembly process down into a series of very basic operations, each of which was entrusted to a specialised worker, who would no longer lose time switching from one task to another. Each movement also had to be simple and effective, and require no thought. As such, Ford organised the various operations into a production line in which the times, pace and positioning of people and machines were studied, with the aim of boosting efficiency and gaining time.

THE MOVING ASSEMBLY LINE

Initially, the workers assembled one car at a time, in a single place to which the pieces, from the chassis to the roof, were brought in stages. However, this approach resulted in a lot of unproductive movement. Ford therefore wanted to reverse the process by bringing the work to the workers.

When the Model N was being manufactured, the workers laid the parts to be assembled out on the floor in the right order, while the car, which was placed on runners and pulled by a rope, advanced from one workstation to the next. This was progress, but it was still not quick enough. Ford then took inspiration from the techniques used to cut up and package meat in abattoirs in Chicago, where the product moved along a rail from one worker to the next, and installed and perfected the first mobile assembly line for automobiles from 1913 onwards. From then on, the workers occupied a fixed post next to a conveyor belt. The parts or cars that were being put together advanced automatically along this conveyor belt, at a speed calculated to optimise output. Thanks to this revolutionary process, the time taken to put together a car was reduced to a quarter of the previous time, which allowed the price of the Model T to be gradually reduced from $825 to $260 (in 1927).

Workers working on the first Ford mobile assembly line in 1913.

This marked the real beginnings of the mass production of

automobiles. In 1913, over 200 000 Model Ts came onto the market, rising to over 300 000 in 1914 and over 500 000 in 1915.

THE MAGIC OF ELECTRICITY

All this organisation would have been impossible without electricity, and above all without electric motors, which were developed from the late 19th century onwards. However, the first factories operated thanks to a central steam engine which set the different mechanisms in motion using a system of pulleys and drive shafts, meaning that it was impossible to conceive of long assembly lines at that time. In 1905, 95% of the machines used in factories still depended on steam engines. By using small electric motors, the engineers at the Ford factory were able to set up the long conveyor belts that made up the assembly line. In the 1920s, electric motors powered half the machines in American factories.

THE FIVE-DOLLAR DAILY WAGE

Nonetheless, the production line had one major disadvantage: it drove away workers, who were quickly put off by the repetitive and monotonous work. In order to maintain a team of 14 000 workers at all times, Ford had to hire an average of 53 000 workers per year. To counter this problem, on 12 January 1914 he decided to double the minimum wage, which rose to five dollars per day (then six dollars in

1919 and seven in 1929), and to establish the eight-hour day. This seemingly risky innovation allowed him to maintain a stable workforce and attract the best workers. In addition, by removing his workers' financial problems (until that point, employers set salaries so as to allow workers the bare minimum needed to live) he greatly improved their productivity, since all their attention and energy were now focused on their work. Against all expectations, Ford therefore managed to reduce production costs.

THE FORD FACTORY

The vast Ford River Rouge Complex in Dearborn, which was built between 1917 and 1928, gradually became home to all the stages of the vehicle manufacturing process, from the transformation of raw materials (metal, glass, rubber, etc.) to the final assembly. This factory, which at one time was the largest in the world, illustrates Ford's ideal vision of rationalised production.

IMPACT

Ford did not invent the automobile or the assembly line, but by perfecting them both he laid the foundations for industry in the 20th century. His innovations had a considerable impact on society and everyday life. It may not even be an exaggeration to say that he is responsible for our current way of life.

A NEW WAY OF LIFE

By creating a car that was accessible to everyone, the Model T, and producing it in very large numbers, Ford enabled all of America to get behind the wheel. Between 1908 and 1927, 15 million cars were produced, and at that time one out of every two American cars was a Model T. In less than two decades, this model completely changed the lives of the population by making it far easier for them to move around. In rural areas, this was a revolutionary development: farms embarked on mechanisation and came out of their isolation, as the Model T not only transported the farmer's family into town, but also allowed them to take their products to market. In addition, later on, tractors made work in the fields easier and faster. Likewise, the Model T enabled faster delivery of goods and services for doctors, carriers and small businessmen.

The Model T, and cars in general, therefore profoundly changed people's daily lives, and also altered the landscape. The number of cars now on the roads necessitated the development of new infrastructures: petrol stations, car parks, better roads and motorways. The influx of travellers also gave rise to restaurants, motels and new tourist attractions.

A REVOLUTIONARY PRODUCTION METHOD

Thanks to his rationalised method of production, which became known as Fordism, Ford gave rise to mass production. This process spread rapidly across industry and became the mode of production which characterised the 20th century. It was applied to everything, from manufacturing phonographs to the production of hamburgers. Since it enabled the production of vast quantities of military material at a speed that Japan and Germany were unable to match, it even indirectly helped the Allies to win the Second World War. It could almost be said that American ships were built more quickly than they could be sunk!

With regard to workers, the impact of Fordism was undoubtedly less positive. Work on the production line required no qualifications, and workers could be trained to do their work in just a few minutes, as demonstrated in Charlie Chaplin's (1889-1977) 1936 film *Modern Times*. This loss of qualifications in labour meant that workers could no longer hope to acquire a skill for life. They were only trained in very precise tasks, depending on their place on the production line. Nonetheless, this did allow the Ford factories to offer work to illiterate immigrants and to the sizeable unskilled workforce resulting from the rural exodus.

The legacy of Fordism

In the last third of the 20th century, the Third Industrial Revolution brought nuclear energy, information technology and electronics. Production lines and Taylorism, which are based on the output of human labour, became obsolete due to the almost complete automatisation of production. The remaining human work in automobile production factories was now carried out by a smaller, versatile and highly trained staff.

THE BEGINNINGS OF MASS CONSUMPTION

Finally, by doubling workers' wages, a practice which spread over time to the rest of the manufacturing industry, Ford contributed to the emergence of a new urban middle class which enjoyed a higher income. The workers could now obtain the cars they produced. In addition, the establishment of the eight-hour day left workers more free time to spend their money.

With the decrease in selling prices resulting from mass production and the increase in purchasing power thanks to salary increases, a new era began: the era of mass consumption, which started in the USA before spreading across the world, and was accompanied by a boom in business services and advertising. In other words, mass production led to mass consumption. Economists describe this process as a virtuous cycle.

SUMMARY

- The movement towards a self-propelled road vehicle (the automobile) began with the invention of Cugnot's *fardier à vapeur*, a large steam-powered carriage, in the 18th century. In the second half of the 19th century, the heavy and inefficient steam engine was replaced by the internal combustion engine, which initially ran on lighting gas, then on petrol. Additionally, the two-stroke engine was replaced by the four-stroke engine, which proved more efficient. While France was initially the world leader in automobile construction, cars became particularly widespread in the USA, thanks to Henry Ford.
- Ford was born in a rural area in 1863, at a time when steam still dominated. He had a passion for machinery, and was particularly interested in the road vehicles that were beginning to appear. After working in various workshops in Detroit, he was taken on as an engineer and machinist at the Edison Illuminating Company, where he worked for nine years, while dedicating his free time to developing a petrol-powered vehicle.
- He left the Edison Illuminating Company to enter the automobile industry in 1899. He secured financial support and, after two unsuccessful attempts, founded the Ford Motor Company. This finally allowed him to make his long-standing aim of building a car that would be accessible to everybody a reality. In 1908, after experimenting for five years, he released the Ford Model T, a simple and sturdy car that experienced consistent success for 19 years.

- To allow every family to purchase a Model T, he strove to boost productivity in his factories in order to regularly reduce the selling price of his car. As such, he put in place a rationalised production system that was intended to save time: he introduced the assembly line to put the cars together, and in 1913 set up the first mobile assembly line, which was controlled by electric motors. From then on, the car that was being put together moved automatically between workstations on a conveyor belt, and the workers remained stationary. This led to a fourfold increase in production.
- To alleviate the monotony of production line work, which was driving workers away, in 1914 Ford decided to double their wages. His initial idea was to make them more productive by taking away their financial worries, but over time this initiative had a larger impact. Through this decision, Ford contributed to the creation of a new social class and ushered in the era of mass consumption.

We want to hear from you!
Leave a comment on your online library
and share your favourite books on social media!

FIND OUT MORE

BIBLIOGRAPHY

- Bellu, S. (1998) *Histoire mondiale de l'automobile*. Paris: Flammarion.
- Eckermann, E. (2001) *World History of the Automobile*. Warrendale: SAE International.
- Ford, H. and Crowther, S. (1922) *My Life and Work*. New York: Garden City Publishing Company.
- Henryford.fr (No date) *Henry Ford*. [Online]. [Accessed 7 March 2017]. Available from: <http://www.henryford.fr/>
- HistoireDuMonde.net (2007) *Henry Ford*. [Online]. [Accessed 7 March 2017]. Available from: <http://www.histoiredumonde.net/Henry-Ford.html>
- History (No date) *Henry Ford*. [Online]. [Accessed 7 March 2017]. Available from: <http://www.history.com/topics/henry-ford>
- Lacey, R. (1986) *Ford*. London: William Heinemann Ltd.
- Lacey, R. (1986) *Ford: The Men and the Machine*. New York: Little, Brown and Company.
- Olson, S. (1963) *Young Henry Ford: A Picture of the First Forty Years*. Detroit: Wayne State University Press.
- Sorensen, C.E. and Williamson, S.T. (1956) *My Forty Years With Ford*. New York: Norton.
- The Henry Ford Heritage Association (No date) *Homepage*. [Online]. [Accessed 7 March 2017]. Available from: <http://hfha.org/>
- Watts, S. (2005) *The People's Tycoon: Henry Ford and the American Century*. New York: A.A. Knopf.

ADDITIONAL SOURCES

- Baldwin, N. (2010) *Henry Ford and the Jews: The Mass Production of Hate*. New York: PublicAffairs.
- Goldstone, L. (2016) *Drive!: Henry Ford, George Selden, and the Race to Invent the Auto Age*. New York: Ballantine Books.
- Snow, R. (2013) *I Invented the Modern Age: The Rise of Henry Ford*. New York: Scribner.

ICONOGRAPHIC SOURCES

- Cugnot's *fardier à vapeur*, drawing by Louis Figuier. Royalty-free reproduction picture.
- Karl Benz's car, dated 1886. Royalty-free reproduction picture.
- Photograph of Ford in his first car, taken in 1896. Royalty-free reproduction picture.
- Photograph of the 999 model with Barney Oldfield in the driver's seat and Ford standing next to him, 1902. Royalty-free reproduction picture.
- Photograph of the first Ford assembly line, 1913. Royalty-free reproduction picture.
- A Ford Model A, dating from 1903. Royalty-free reproduction picture.
- Photograph of a couple in a Ford Model N, taken by William Creswell in 1906. Royalty-free reproduction picture.
- Ford posing next to the Model T, 1921. Royalty-free reproduction picture.
- Workers working on the first Ford mobile assembly line

in 1913. Royalty-free reproduction picture.

FILMS AND DOCUMENTARIES

- *Modern Times*. (1936) [Film]. Charlie Chaplin. Dir. USA: Charles Chaplin Productions.
- *Henry Ford*, 2013. American Experience. [Television programme]. PBS, 29 January 2013.

IMPROVE YOUR GENERAL KNOWLEDGE
IN A BLINK OF AN EYE !
www.50minutes.com

© **50MINUTES.com, 2016. All rights reserved.**

www.50minutes.com

Ebook EAN: 9782806293909

Paperback EAN: 9782806294524

Legal Deposit: D/2017/12603/115

Cover: © Primento

Digital conception by Primento, the digital partner of publishers.

Made in the USA
Monee, IL
07 July 2026

56545373R00024